NATIONAL GEOGRAPHIC KiDS

Funny FILL-IN

MY BUG ADVENTURE

NATIONAL GEOGRAPHIC
WASHINGTON, D.C.

How to Play Funny Fill-In!

Love to create amazing stories? Good, because this one stars YOU. Get ready to laugh with all your friends—you can play with as many people as you want! Make sure to keep this book on your shelf. You'll want to read it again and again!

Are You Ready to Laugh?

- One person picks a story—you can start at the beginning, the middle, or the end of the book.

- Ask a friend to call out a word that the space asks for—noun, verb, or something else—and write it in the blank space. If there's more than one player, ask the next person to say a word. Extra points for creativity!

- When all the spaces are filled in, you have your very own Funny Fill-In. Read it out loud for a laugh.

- Want to play by yourself? Just fold over the page and use the cardboard insert at the back as a writing pad. Fill in the blank parts of speech list, and copy your answers into the story.

Make sure you check out the amazing **Fun Facts** that appear on every page!

To play the game, you'll need to know how to form sentences. This list with examples of the parts of speech and other terms will help you get started:

Noun: The name of a person, place, thing, or idea
Examples: tree, mouth, creature
The ocean is full of colorful fish.

Adjective: A word that describes a noun or pronoun
Examples: green, lazy, friendly
My silly dog won't stop laughing!

Verb: An action word. In the present tense, a verb often ends in –s or –ing. If the space asks for past tense, changing the vowel or adding a –d or –ed to the end usually will set the sentence in the past.
Examples: swim, hide, plays, running (present tense); biked, rode, jumped (past tense)
The giraffe skips across the savanna.
The flower opened after the rain.

Adverb: A word that describes a verb and usually ends in –ly
Examples: quickly, lazily, soundlessly
Kelley greedily ate all the carrots.

Plural: More than one
Examples: mice, telephones, wrenches
Why are all the doors closing?

Silly Word or Exclamation: A funny sound, a made-up word, a word you think is totally weird, or a noise someone or something might make
Examples: Ouch! No way! Foozleduzzle! Yikes!
"Darn!" shouted Jim. "These cupcakes are sour!"

Specific Words: There are many more ways to make your story hilarious. When asked for something like a number, animal, or body part, write in something you think is especially funny.

- friend's name
  - adjective
- type of vehicle
  - name that starts with *B*
- type of insect, plural
  - same type of insect
- type of insect, plural
  - noun, plural
- noun
  - silly word
- same friend's name
  - adjective
- noun
  - noun, plural
- clothing item, plural
  - adjective
- nickname
  - something shiny
- type of animal

BUG EMPORIUM

CLOSED

CLOSED
DUE TO
MISSIN
BUGS

Fun Fact! There are about 10 quintillion bugs on Earth. That's 1.4 billion bugs for every one human!

Bug Hunters

__Yami__ and I are __Snowy__ . We're in my family's __mini van__ on the way
friend's name · *adjective* · *type of vehicle*

to __Ben__ 's Big Bug Emporium to get __ants__ to make a(n) __ant__
name that starts with B · *type of insect, plural* · *same type of insect*

farm. It's my favorite store in the whole town. Last year I bought __butterflies__ that grew as large
type of insect, plural

as __fences__ there! But when we get to the store, we see a large __bush__ next to the door
noun, plural · *noun*

with "Closed Due to Missing Bugs" written on it. Oh, __burp__ ! But then __Yanni__ gets
silly word · *same friend's name*

a(n) __warm__ look on his/her face and pulls a(n) __village, villages__ , and
adjective · *noun* · *noun, plural*

__shoes__ from his/her backpack and puts them on. " __silly__
clothing item, plural · *adjective*

thinking, __D'Vick__ ," I say and get out my magnifying __Jewlery__
nickname · *something shiny*

and my __horse__ net. Bug Hunters to the rescue!
type of animal

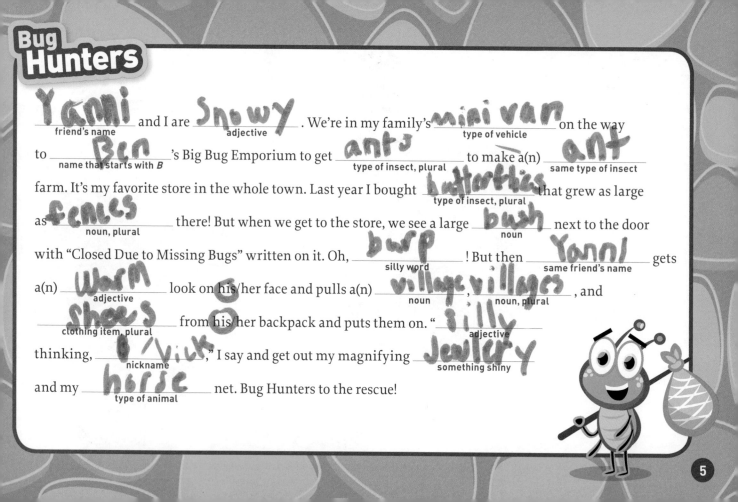

5

- feeling
  - noun, plural
- noun
  - verb
- noun
  - same noun
- number
  - family member's name
- type of animal
  - noun
- verb ending in –ed
  - number
- adverb ending in –ly
  - adjective ending in –est
- verb
  - type of insect
- verb ending in –ing
  - adjective
- same verb ending in –ing

BUG EMPORIUM

BUG EMPORIUM

BUG FOOD

BUG FOOD

Fun Fact! In 2007, a cockroach named Nadezhda was the first creature to conceive in space. She later gave birth to 33 baby cockroaches.

Crabby Cockroaches

The store manager looks _____HAPPY_____ (feeling) to see us, so I ask if we can look around. We search under the _____cars_____ (noun, plural) and inside a large _____hair_____ (noun). But just when we think there are no bugs left anywhere,

we see something scuttle past and _____running_____ (verb) under a(n) _____grandpa_____ (noun). We lift up the _____grandpa_____ (same noun) and

see bugs with _____5 ½ or 10_____ (number) leg(s). I know what these bugs are because when _____maddie_____ (family member's name) sees them in

our house, he/she screams like a baby _____onion_____ (type of animal). But I don't mind cockroaches, so I take out my

writing _____tail_____ (noun) and get down to business. "When is the last time you _____stealed_____ (verb ending in –ed)?" I ask. But

the cockroaches just hiss at me. So I try again: "Where were you at _____65_____ (number) o'clock today?" They look at

me _____searcardy_____ (adverb ending in –ly). Finally the _____stupidest_____ (adjective ending in –est) one takes pity on me and says, "If you want to

_____jog_____ (verb) like a(n) _____butterfly_____ (type of insect), you have to be smarter and better at _____flying_____ (verb ending in –ing) than it is."

This will be _____ignoring_____ (adjective), I think. I'm better at _____joging_____ (same verb ending in –ing) than anybody—I mean any bug!

verb

    friend's name

noun

    adjective

body part, plural

    type of food, plural

noun, plural

    noun, plural

noun

    body part

exclamation

    same body part

type of food

    body part

noun

    something slimy, plural

something wet, plural

    verb

 Fun Fact! Flies taste not only with their mouthparts, but also with tiny hairs on their feet.

"The first thing we need to do is _____ around the perimeter," _____ says.
                                    verb   friend's name

So we each grab a(n) _____ and head outside. That's when we smell something really
                        noun

_____ . We follow our _____ to a Dumpster behind the building. Inside we find
adjective   body part, plural

rotting _____ , used _____ , and broken _____ . A fly lands next to us on .
        type of food, plural   noun, plural   noun, plural

a(n) _____ . "Mmmm," it says, walking all over it. "Use your _____ and taste this."
        noun   body part

" _____ !" I say, putting my _____ on a(n) _____ . But I can't taste
   exclamation   same body part   type of food

anything. Then my friend tries, putting his/her _____ on a(n) _____ . But when he/she
                                                 body part   noun

does, _____ and _____ squirt out everywhere, even onto me! "Don't worry,
      something slimy, plural something wet, plural

we'll have this cleaned up in a jiffy," says the fly, calling the other flies to _____ all over us. When
                                                                                  verb

they finish, we're all spick-and-span and ready to find bugs!

number

verb

adjective

body part

body part

friend's name

famous athlete

gymnastics move

clothing item

adjective

color

noun, plural

noun, plural

noun, plural

type of structure

adverb ending in –ly

same type of structure

noun

adverb ending in –ly

Fun Fact! Flea circuses used to be a form of entertainment in which fleas were dressed in tiny clothing and made to do tricks.

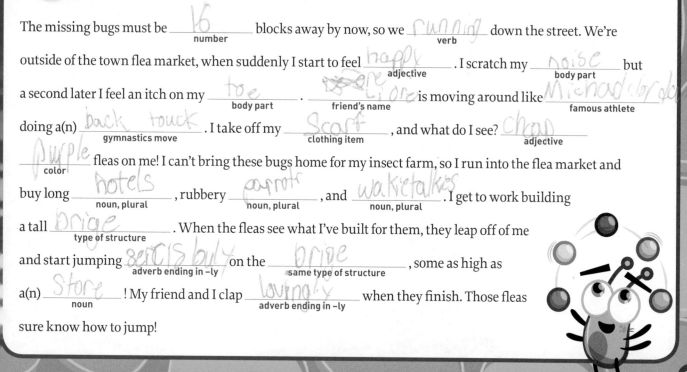

Jump Right Up!

The missing bugs must be ___16___ [number] blocks away by now, so we ___running___ [verb] down the street. We're

outside of the town flea market, when suddenly I start to feel ___happy___ [adjective]. I scratch my ___noise___ [body part] but

a second later I feel an itch on my ___toe___ [body part]. ___~~store~~ Liore___ [friend's name] is moving around like ___Michael Jordan___ [famous athlete]

doing a(n) ___back touch___ [gymnastics move]. I take off my ___scarf___ [clothing item], and what do I see? ___cheap___ [adjective]

___purple___ [color] fleas on me! I can't bring these bugs home for my insect farm, so I run into the flea market and

buy long ___hotels___ [noun, plural], rubbery ___parrots___ [noun, plural], and ___walkietalkies___ [noun, plural]. I get to work building

a tall ___brige___ [type of structure]. When the fleas see what I've built for them, they leap off of me

and start jumping ___sericsbuly___ [adverb ending in –ly] on the ___brige___ [same type of structure], some as high as

a(n) ___store___ [noun]! My friend and I clap ___lovingly___ [adverb ending in –ly] when they finish. Those fleas

sure know how to jump!

adjective

   type of animal, plural

friend's name

   feeling

noun, plural

   noun, plural

adjective ending in –er

   same adjective ending in –er

adjective

   type of instrument

same friend's name

   body part, plural

noun

   famous pop star

silly word

   verb

something sparkly

   feeling

Fun Fact! Male cicadas use a body part on their abdomens called a tymbal to make a "song" to attract a female.

Cicada Swoon

We decide to drop the fleas off in a(n) _____ (adjective) area where they'll be able to find lots of _____ (type of animal, plural) to live on. Just as we're saying goodbye to our new friends, we hear an eerie noise.

At first _____ (friend's name) and I are _____ (feeling) because we can't figure out where the sound is coming from. We look under leafy _____ (noun, plural) and flip over _____ (noun, plural) on the ground, but we don't see anything. Then the noise starts getting _____ (adjective ending in –er) and _____ (same adjective ending in –er). It's as loud as a(n) _____ (adjective) _____ (type of instrument)! _____ (same friend's name) covers his/her _____ (body part, plural), and I pull my _____ (noun) over my head. But then the noise starts to sound like _____ (famous pop star) singing the song "_____ (silly word), Let's _____ (verb) Together." Cool! "Turn it up louder!" we say. Just then we see female cicadas start to emerge from the trees and head toward the music with _____ (something sparkly) in their eyes. *Awww.* We don't want to capture these bugs while there is so much _____ (feeling) in the air!

loud noise

verb ending in –ing

noun, plural

friend's name

body part

adjective

noun

adjective

same noun

clothing item

noun

noun

verb

verb

verb

feeling

dance move

Fun Fact!

The Chan's megastick is the longest insect in the world, at about 22 inches (56 cm) long—more than twice as long as this book is

Stick'em Up!

Suddenly we hear a(n) _____ ! It sounds like _____ _____ . We follow
the noise to a tree. At first we don't see anything. Then we hear it again. That's when _____
points his/her _____ and says, "Look over there, two _____ stick insects are having
a(n) _____ duel." "En garde!" says one of them, pointing a(n) _____ _____ at us.
His opponent, who is wearing a leafy _____ , says, "You dirty _____ ," and brandishes
a large _____ . We start to _____ slowly away from the dueling insects, but then
the leaves on the branches begin to _____ and _____ . That's when I see that
they're alive too! The leaf bugs are _____ when the stick bugs do a spectacular
_____ and then bow. It was all an act! Whew, what a great show!

(labels under blanks, in order: loud noise; verb ending in –ing; noun, plural; friend's name; body part; adjective; noun; adjective; same noun; clothing item; noun; noun; verb; verb; verb; feeling; dance move)

type of insect, plural

color

color

body part, plural

verb

verb ending in –ing

noun

color

adjective

verb

adverb ending in –ly

noun

friend's name

same type of insect, plural

noun

verb

unit of time

same friend's name

part of a flower

16

Fun Fact! Butterflies see more colors and patterns than humans do because they can see ultraviolet light.

Busy Bugs

The stick bugs and leaf bugs put on a great show, but we need to keep looking for _____ (type of insect, plural).

We come across a meadow filled with _____ (color) and _____ (color) flowers as far as our _____ (body part, plural)

can _____ (verb). We must have hit the jackpot because there are bugs everywhere! Wasps are

_____ (verb ending in –ing) with bees over _____ (noun) flowers. Tiny _____ (color) ants are crawling all over

_____ (adjective) flower petals, while beetles _____ (verb) _____ (adverb ending in –ly) up the stems. Suddenly

a butterfly with _____ (noun)-patterned wings flies by. "Excuse me," _____ (friend's name) says, "are there

any _____ (same type of insect, plural) around here?" But I guess the butterflies are too distracted by the

flowers to talk to us. I take out my _____ (noun) net and prepare to _____ (verb), but my friend

says, "Hold on a(n) _____ (unit of time). If we capture these bugs, we'll hurt the flowers." I guess

he/she is right. Good thing _____ (same friend's name) nipped my idea in the _____ (part of a flower).

17

color

color

adjective

verb

noun

adjective

noun, plural

same noun, plural

noun

verb ending in –ing

number

adjective

type of profession

type of food

type of food

Fun Fact! Honeybees are overachievers—they make and store two to three times more food than they need.

Don't Sweat the Sweet Stuff

A swarm of flying insects with _____ (color) and _____ (color) stripes is heading straight at us. Honeybees!

I hope they don't want to sting us with their _____ (adjective) stingers. But the bees _____ (verb) right past us and

into a(n) _____ (noun). That must be where their honey is. If we can get them to come home with us, then we

could have all the _____ (adjective) honey we want! Beekeepers use _____ (noun, plural) to get bees to leave

the hives so they can harvest the honeycombs, but we don't have any _____ (same noun, plural) in our backpacks.

We try singing "Sweet _____ (noun) of Mine," but that doesn't attract the bees. Then we try _____ (verb ending in –ing)

around the hive, but the bees just ignore us. After _____ (number) minute(s), we're _____ (adjective) from trying.

Good thing we can just stop by the _____ (type of profession) 's market on the way home

and buy a honey-coated _____ (type of food) or a honeyed _____ (type of food) instead.

HONEY

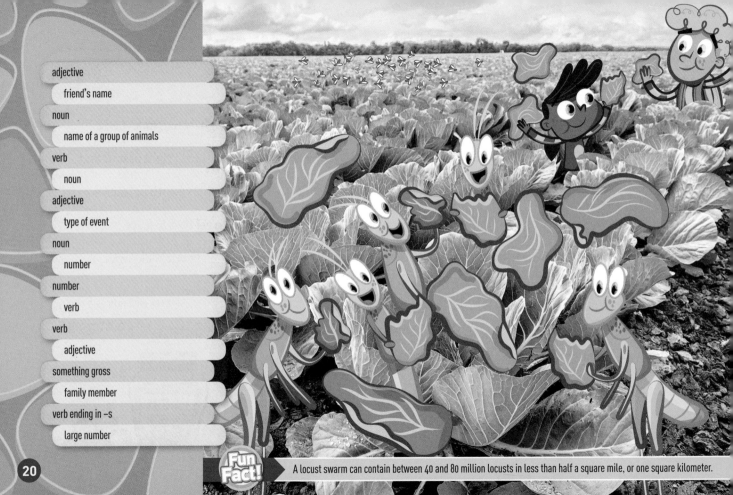

adjective

    friend's name

noun

    name of a group of animals

verb

    noun

adjective

    type of event

noun

    number

number

    verb

verb

    adjective

something gross

    family member

verb ending in –s

    large number

Fun Fact! A locust swarm can contain between 40 and 80 million locusts in less than half a square mile, or one square kilometer.

Vege-terrible

The sky darkens and _____ clouds appear. _____ and I grab a(n) _____ to
                       adjective   friend's name   noun

put over our heads and run for cover. But those aren't rain clouds at all—it's a huge _____
                                                                                       name of a group of animals

of locusts coming out of the sky. The locusts _____ onto a leafy _____ and start munching.
                                                verb   noun

When the locusts fly away, the leaves are all gone! That's when I get a(n) _____ idea. Eating contest!
                                                                            adjective

Last year at the _____ , I won first place in a(n) _____ -eating contest. So I ask the nearest locust
                  type of event   noun

to compete with me, and it says yes. We decide to see who can eat _____ plant(s) in _____ second(s)
                                                                   number   number

to see who wins. "Ready, set, _____ !" my friend says. I _____ as much as I can, but I start to
                               verb   verb

feel _____ right away. These plants taste like the _____ that my _____ makes.
      adjective   something gross   family member

My locust opponent _____ like a pro, and I lose the contest. If we captured these bugs, it would
                    verb ending in –s

cost us _____ dollars just to feed them!
         large number

- noun
  - adjective
- noun, plural
  - color
- large number
  - noun, plural
- type of animal
  - body part, plural
- noun, plural
  - adjective
- friend's name
  - body part
- verb
  - noun
- same friend's name
  - noun, plural
- verb
  - number
- number

Fun Fact!

The taurus scarab, a type of dung beetle, is the world's strongest insect. It can pull an object 1,141 times heavier than itself.

After the locusts fly off, the ground looks as barren as a(n) _____ . But then we see something
noun

really _____ ! Hiding under green _____ and _____ branches are beetles—
adjective _noun, plural_ _color_

_____ of them. When we get closer, we see the beetles are carrying heavy _____ on
large number _noun, plural_

their backs and rolling huge balls of _____ dung. I'm superstrong, with _____ as
type of animal _body part, plural_

big as _____ , and the beetles agree that if we can beat them in a(n) _____ weight-lifting
noun, plural _adjective_

competition, then we get to take them home with us. _____ hops onto my _____ , and
friend's name _body part_

we get ready to _____ to the nearest _____ and back. But _____ must have eaten
verb _noun_ _same friend's name_

too many _____ because he/she is heavy. We only get a couple of steps before we _____
noun, plural _verb_

to the ground. The winning beetle carries _____ other beetle(s) on its back and finishes the race
number

in _____ second(s) flat. That's when I get an idea. I'll ask the beetles to give us a ride!
number

- type of animal
  - adjective
- type of structure
  - number
- adjective
  - noun, plural
- something stinky, plural
  - large number
- noun, plural
  - body part, plural
- clothing item, plural
  - verb ending in –ing
- feeling
  - adjective
- large number
  - noun
- verb
  - friend's name
- body part, plural

Fun Fact! Termite queens produce about 20 eggs a minute.

Termite Entourage

The beetles give us a(n) _____ (type of animal) -back ride and drop us off at a(n) _____ (adjective) _____ (type of structure)

that is as tall as a(n) _____ (number) -story building. We're not sure what it is, but it appears _____ (adjective) ,

like it was built out of sawdust, _____ (noun, plural) , and _____ (something stinky, plural) . Suddenly _____ (large number)

termites stream out from holes in the side of the mound. Some of them are carrying _____ (noun, plural) on

their _____ (body part, plural) , while others are wearing what look like _____ (clothing item, plural) . It appears

that we interrupted them while they were _____ (verb ending in –ing) , and they don't look too _____ (feeling)

about it. But then the queen appears. She's so _____ (adjective) that _____ (large number) workers

carry her on a(n) _____ (noun) . The termites all _____ (verb) down in front of her,

so _____ (friend's name) and I get down on our _____ (body part, plural) and do the same.

All hail the queen!

25

verb

    type of insect, plural

adjective

    something stinky

type of food

    body part, plural

color

    type of liquid

body part, plural

    adjective

family member, plural

    type of pet, plural

adjective

    family member

noun

    noun

feeling

    verb

Fun Fact! Some stink bugs secrete a chemical that smells like skunk when they are threatened.

Eau de Stink Bug

After the royal show, we _____ (verb) around to see if we can find _____ (type of insect, plural). Whoa, what's that _____ (adjective) smell? It smells like _____ (something stinky) and old _____ (type of food) mixed together. We follow our _____ (body part, plural) to the source of the smell. There, we find flat _____ (color) bugs that are making perfume from _____ (type of liquid) that comes from their _____ (body part, plural). They ask us if we want a(n) _____ (adjective) sample. "Your _____ (family member, plural) and _____ (type of pet, plural) will go _____ (adjective) for it," they promise us. Last year I got my _____ (family member) a(n) _____ (noun) for his/her birthday, but I don't think he/she liked it much, because I found it under a(n) _____ (noun) in the closet. So this will make him/her _____ (feeling) for sure! But when I take a big whiff, it makes me want to _____ (verb). Pee-ew! I don't want these stinky bugs coming home with me.

verb ending in –ing

noun

adjective

something shiny, plural

adjective

clothing item

noun, plural

noun

noun, plural

noun

same noun

something sticky

body part, plural

friend's name

color

body part, plural

adjective

noun

adjective

Fun Fact! The secret of silkmaking was so valuable in ancient China that smuggling silkworms out of the country was punishable by death.

Silkworm Secrets

We keep _____ until we come to a(n) _____ . Hanging all around it is _____
verb ending in –ing _noun_ _adjective_

cloth that shimmers like _____ . We hear a voice say, "How about a(n) _____
something shiny, plural _adjective_

_____ to go with your pretty _____ ?" When we peek behind a(n) _____ ,
clothing item _noun, plural_ _noun_

we see silkworm moths making large cloth _____ . We ask if we can help. The first thing
noun, plural

we have to do is unravel the empty silkworm cocoons _____ by _____ to make thread,
noun _same noun_

but when we do, _____ gets all over our _____ . The next step is to dye the
something sticky _body part, plural_

threads, but _____ and I end up with _____ _____ instead.
friend's name _color_ _body part, plural_

We try weaving the threads together, but our cloth comes out looking more like

a(n) _____ _____ ! We leave these bugs to do their _____ work,
adjective _noun_ _adjective_

and we slip away.

29

- feeling
  - verb
- body part, plural
  - verb ending in –s
- verb ending in –ing
  - body part, plural
- body part, plural
  - dance move
- famous pop star
  - friend's name
- verb ending in –s
  - verb
- noun
  - verb ending in –ing
- type of animal
  - number
- noise
  - same friend's name
- adverb ending in –ly

Fun Fact! Mantids can turn their heads 180 degrees.

Meditating Mantis

We're _____ from our bug hunt, so we decide to _____ for a little while beside
feeling   _verb_

some trees. That's when we notice a tiny statue that is holding its _____ together
body part, plural

like it is praying. Suddenly it _____. A praying mantis! We ask what it's doing, and it
verb ending in –s

says it's _____ and we can join in. All we have to do is cross our _____
verb ending in –ing   _body part, plural_

over our _____ then _____ like _____. The praying mantis
body part, plural   _dance move_   _famous pop star_

demonstrates, but when we try and do the same thing, _____ _____ right into
friend's name   _verb ending in –s_

me. I _____ through the air right into a(n) _____. The praying mantis sighs and tells us to
verb   _noun_

try _____ and humming quietly like a(n) _____ for _____ minute(s)
verb ending in –ing   _type of animal_   _number_

instead. We try, but I _____ loudly and _____ starts to giggle. The mantis looks at
noise   _same friend's name_

us _____ and hops away.
adverb ending in –ly

- verb ending in –ing
- large number
- noun, plural
- name of a place
- adjective
- verb
- friend's name
- adjective
- verb
- number
- name of a body of water
- verb
- large number
- verb
- time of year

Fun Fact! Monarch butterflies from eastern North America migrate up to 3,000 miles (4,828 km) to get to their winter home in Mexico.

Come Fly With Us

There's nothing to do but keep _____ . We don't get too far when suddenly
verb ending in –ing

we are surrounded by _____ monarch butterflies with orange and black markings
large number

in the shape of _____ . They tell us they are all going to _____ for
noun, plural   *name of a place*

a(n) _____ vacation and ask if we want to _____ along with them. Why
adjective   *verb*

not, _____ and I decide. All this bug hunting has been _____ work so far.
friend's name   *adjective*

We _____ after the butterflies for _____ minute(s) until we come to _____ .
verb   *number*   *name of a body of water*

We can't _____ over the water like the butterflies can. "Come on," they call to us. "There are
verb

only _____ hours left to go." But we can't go that far—we have a bug hunt to finish! So
large number

we _____ and call out to the butterflies as they fly away, "See you next _____ !"
verb   *time of year*

MEXICO OR BUST

- friend's name
  - verb
- noun
  - verb
- number, plural
  - verb
- verb
  - your age
- dance move
  - type of animal, plural
- same friend's name
  - adverb ending in –ly
- verb
  - noun
- number
  - same noun
- same noun, plural
  - feeling

Fun Fact! A water strider's middle legs push it forward, while the hind legs help it to steer.

Skillful Striders

_____ and I _____ down by the water, wondering what to do next. That is, until we see
  friend's name   verb

the water striders having a(n) _____-skating competition. Two bugs _____ toward each other,
                    noun   verb

then twirl in perfect figure-_____. The other bugs _____ and _____ as three
                  number, plural   verb   verb

more bugs join the skaters. Finally, _____ more appear and _____ across the
                        your age   dance move

water as gracefully as _____. Then they all stop and look at _____ and me
                  type of animal, plural   same friend's name

_____. Do they want us to _____ with them? Suddenly I get an idea. I open my backpack
adverb ending in –ly   verb

and take out a marker and a(n) _____. I write a big number _____ on the _____ and
                    noun   number   same noun

get my friend to do the same. We hold up our _____ at the same
                        same noun, plural

time, and the crowd of water striders gets _____. A perfect score!
                        feeling

- adjective ending in –est
  - verb
- noun
  - verb ending in –s
- gymnastics move
  - noun, plural
- number
  - noun
- exclamation
  - large number
- noun, plural
  - body part
- verb
  - verb ending in –s
- noun
  - something sparkly
- adjective
  - noun, plural

Fun Fact! Some diving beetles collect and store air under their wings so they can breathe underwater.

Just when we think the show is over, the diving beetles come out. The ＿＿＿＿＿＿＿＿＿＿
adjective ending in –est

thing about them is how they can ＿＿＿＿＿＿ while underwater. A beetle the size of
verb

a(n) ＿＿＿＿＿ ＿＿＿＿＿＿＿ off a branch, does a(n) ＿＿＿＿＿＿＿＿＿ , and dives into
noun _verb ending in –s_ _gymnastics move_

the water. We all hold our ＿＿＿＿＿＿ for ＿＿＿＿＿ second(s) before it appears at the surface
noun, plural _number_

again. When it does, it is holding a large shiny ＿＿＿＿＿ . ＿＿＿＿＿＿ , where did that come from?
noun _exclamation_

The next beetle has ＿＿＿＿＿＿ ＿＿＿＿＿＿ on its ＿＿＿＿＿ . It can hardly ＿＿＿＿＿ , but it
large number _noun, plural_ _body part_ _verb_

still ＿＿＿＿＿＿ into the water like a famous ＿＿＿＿＿ . When it comes back up, it also has
verb ending in –s _noun_

a(n) ＿＿＿＿＿＿ . There must be ＿＿＿＿＿＿ treasure down there. Too bad we didn't bring our
something sparkly _adjective_

diving ＿＿＿＿＿＿ !
noun, plural

- friend's name
  - adjective
- verb
  - adjective
- adjective
  - type of building
- same friend's name
  - adjective
- type of lizard, plural
  - verb
- type of insect, plural
  - noun, plural
- noun, plural
  - type of animal, plural
- sound
  - verb
- verb

Fun Fact! Griffinflies are an ancient—and gigantic—relative of dragonflies that lived about 300 million years ago.

Dragon Tales

_____ and I have had a(n) _____ day, but we need a rest. We _____
friend's name   adjective   verb

under a tree just in time to hear an old, _____ dragonfly invite his _____ baby
                                                              adjective   adjective

dragonflies, called nymphs, to hear a story. I love story time at my local _____ ,
                                                                                                              type of building

so _____ and I gather around, too. The dragonfly tells us of his ancient ancestor
      same friend's name

_____-Heart the Flyer, who lived during the time of the great _____ and
adjective   type of lizard, plural

had to _____ giant _____ and hairy _____ just to survive.
            verb   type of insect, plural   noun, plural

Way back then, he tells us, there were plants as large as _____ and fish as fierce as
                                                                                    noun, plural

a(n) _____ . The young nymphs _____ and _____ .
        type of animal, plural   sound   verb

Me? I'm just glad I didn't _____ way back then!
                                        verb

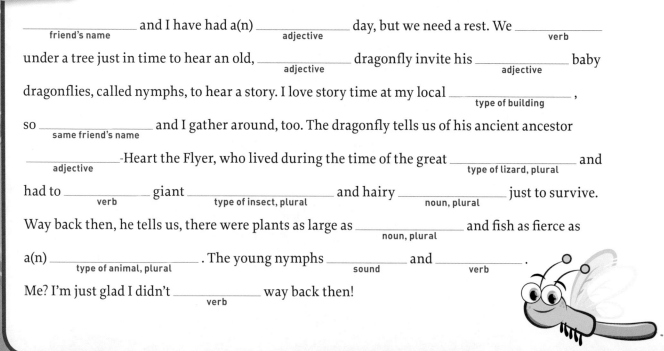

- your favorite food
  - adjective ending in –y
- friend's name
  - noun
- noun
  - verb
- type of profession
  - verb ending in –s
- nickname, plural
  - type of animal, plural
- adjective
  - verb
- adverb ending in –ly
  - same favorite food
- name of a holiday
  - same favorite food

Fun Fact! Farmers like ladybugs because they eat aphids, which destroy crops.

Ladybug Luck

We finally make our way to a farmer's field, where _____ is growing. And what do we
                                                    your favorite food

see? Tons and tons of ladybugs. They say ladybugs are _____ , and I guess they're right.
                                                        adjective ending in –y

We'll be able to catch a lot of bugs and keep them as pets! _____ and I get ready to catch them
                                                              friend's name

with our _____ nets and _____ jars. But just then we hear a voice call, "_____ !" A(n)
          noun   *noun*   *verb*

_____ in overalls _____ up to us. "You can't take my_____ . They
type of profession   *verb ending in –s*   *nickname, plural*

eat the tiny _____ that eat my _____ plants." My friend and I _____ at
              type of animal, plural   *adjective*   *verb*

each other _____ and drop our nets and jars. No more _____ ? I guess we
            adverb ending in –ly   *same favorite food*

will leave the ladybugs where they are and move on. What would _____ parties
                                                                name of a holiday

be without _____ ?
            same favorite food

body part

verb

adjective

noun

adjective

color

friend's name

verb ending in –s

silly word

noun

verb ending in –ed

adjective

verb ending in –ing

same verb ending in –ing

verb

number

adverb ending in –ly

42

Fun Fact! Scientists have observed that moths don't rest just anywhere on tree bark; they find the spot where they blend in the best.

Masquerading Moths

We enter into a wooded area. Out of the corner of my _____ , I see something _____ .

body part / verb

"Was that a(n) _____ _____ ?" I ask my friend. I guess not, because everything is still.

adjective / noun

So we keep walking past _____ _____ trees. Suddenly _____ _____

adjective / color / friend's name / verb ending in –s

and says, "Look, _____ , that _____ just _____ !" Sure enough, when we look

silly word / noun / verb ending in –ed

closer we see _____ moths _____ . But then the moths are still. They blend in so

adjective / verb ending in –ing

well with the trees that when they stop _____ we can't see them anymore.

same verb ending in –ing

"Let's play hide-and-_____ with them," I say. We count to _____ to give the

verb / number

moths a chance to hide. But when we go to look for them, we can't find them

anymore. Have they blended in so _____ , or have they disappeared?

adverb ending in –ly

silly word

adverb ending in –ly

verb ending in –s

your age

body part, plural

body part, plural

verb

adjective

verb ending in –s

adverb

noun

adjective

body part, plural

same body part, plural

sound

verb

adjective

44

Fun Fact!

Crickets use their powerful hind legs to jump up to 30 times their own body length into the air.

"Watch out, _____ ," my friend says _____ and _____ me to the ground.
          silly word   adverb ending in –ly   verb ending in –s

_____ crickets appear right before my _____ ! It looks like they're getting ready for
  your age   body part, plural

a jumping competition! So we get down on our _____ and get ready to _____ . Just
                                              body part, plural   verb

then a(n) _____ cricket _____ into the air. I jump as _____ as I can, but
          adjective   verb ending in –s   adverb

I only get as high as a(n) _____ . "Try using your _____ _____ to jump, like
                           noun   adjective   body part, plural

the crickets," my friend says. Good idea, I think, and I try to use my _____ , but I end up
                                                                       same body part, plural

landing on the ground with a loud _____ . I decide to just _____ on the ground for a while,
                                  sound   verb

enjoying the _____ sunset and watching the crickets jump into the air.
             adjective

friend's name

    noun

adjective

    adjective

noun

    verb

body part, plural

    noun, plural

same friend's name

    noun

verb

    noun

letter of the alphabet

    type of animal

nickname

    noun

number

Fun Fact! Different species of fireflies have their own distinct "flash fingerprints."

Seeing the Light

It's almost dark out. _____ and I are lying on a(n) _____ looking up at the sky. We see
　　　　　　　　　friend's name　　　　　　　　　　　　　　　　noun

_____ lights above. We're trying to find the _____ Dipper when suddenly the lights start
adjective　　　　　　　　　　　　　　　　　　　　　adjective

to come closer and closer. "Watch out, it's an alien _____ coming to _____ us!" my friend
　　　　　　　　　　　　　　　　　　　　　　　　noun　　　　　　　　verb

shrieks. But it's only fireflies lighting up their _____ to try and attract _____.
　　　　　　　　　　　　　　　　　　　　body part, plural　　　　　　　　　　noun, plural

"We could catch them for our insect farm," _____ says, getting out a(n) _____.
　　　　　　　　　　　　　　　　　　same friend's name　　　　　　　　　　noun

But then the fireflies _____ into a(n) _____ shape in the sky. We laugh as they move into
　　　　　　　　　verb　　　　　　　noun

a(n) _____ formation, followed by a(n) _____ shape. "You know,
　　letter of the alphabet　　　　　　　　　　type of animal

_____," I say to my friend, putting down my bug-hunting _____, "I think
nickname　　　　　　　　　　　　　　　　　　　　　　　　noun

we should just leave all the bugs in nature, where they belong. " We high-_____ and
　　　　　　　　　　　　　　　　　　　　　　　　　　　　number

follow the fireflies as they light our path home.

Credits

Cover, NomadSoul1/iStock; 4, Mark Winfrey/Shutterstock; 6, Olga Koronevska/iStock; 8, Narongrit Dantragoon/Shutterstock; 10, Little NY/Shutterstock; 12, Joop Snijder Photography/Shutterstock; 14, Triff/Shutterstock; 16, Chain Foto 24/Shutterstock; 18, Fotolotti/Dreamstime; 20, S-F/Shutterstock; 22, Ivana Vrnoga/Shutterstock; 24, Jakkrit Orrasri/Shutterstock; 26, Kingarion/Shutterstock; 28, Sergei Kazakov/Shutterstock; 30, Liusheng Film/Shutterstock; 32, Jean-Edouard Rozey/Shutterstock; 34, Greir/Shutterstock; 36, Vasin Lee/Shutterstock; 38, Zephyr P./Shutterstock; 40, Fotokostic/Shutterstock; 42, Aleksander Bolbot/Shutterstock; 42, Patrick Foto/Shutterstock; 46, Anekoho/Shutterstock

Staff for This Book

Ariane Szu-Tu, *Project Editor*
James Hiscott, Jr. and Callie Broaddus,
    Art Directors
Kelley Miller, *Senior Photo Editor*
Carrie Gleason, *Writer*
Jason Tharp, *Illustrator*
Paige Towler, *Editorial Assistant*
Sanjida Rashid and Rachel Kenny, *Design
    Production Assistants*
Tammi Colleary-Loach, *Rights Clearance Manager*
Michael Cassady and Mari Robinson, *Rights
    Clearance Specialists*
Grace Hill, *Managing Editor*
Joan Gossett, *Senior Production Editor*
Lewis R. Bassford, *Production Manager*
Jenn Hoff, *Manager, Production Services*
Susan Borke, *Legal and Business Affairs*

Published by the National Geographic Society

Gary E. Knell, *President and CEO*
John M. Fahey, *Chairman of the Board*
Melina Gerosa Bellows, *Chief Education Officer*
Declan Moore, *Chief Media Officer*
Hector Sierra, *Senior Vice President and General
    Manager, Book Division*

Senior Management Team, Kids Publishing and Media

Nancy Laties Feresten, *Senior Vice President*
Erica Green, *Vice President, Editorial Director,
    Kids Books*
Julie Vosburgh Agnone, *Vice President, Operations*
Jennifer Emmett, *Vice President, Content*
Michelle Sullivan, *Vice President, Video and Digital
    Initiatives*
Eva Absher-Schantz, *Vice President, Visual Identity*
Rachel Buchholz, *Editor and Vice President*, NG
    Kids *magazine*
Jay Sumner, *Photo Director*
Hannah August, *Marketing Director*
R. Gary Colbert, *Production Director*

Digital

Laura Goertzel, *Manager*
Sara Zeglin, *Senior Producer*
Bianca Bowman, *Assistant Producer*
Natalie Jones, *Senior Product Manager*

Editorial, Design, and Production by Plan B Book Packagers

The National Geographic Society is one of the world's largest nonprofit scientific and educational organizations. Founded in 1888 to "increase and diffuse geographic knowledge," the Society's mission is to inspire people to care about the planet. It reaches more than 400 million people worldwide each month through its official journal, *National Geographic*, and other magazines; National Geographic Channel; television documentaries; music; radio; films; books; DVDs; maps; exhibitions; live events; school publishing programs; interactive media; and merchandise. National Geographic has funded more than 10,000 scientific research, conservation, and exploration projects and supports an education program promoting geographic literacy.

For more information, please visit nationalgeographic.com, call 1-800-NGS LINE (647-5463), or write to the following address:

National Geographic Society, 1145 17th Street N.W.
Washington, D.C. 20036-4688 U.S.A.

Visit us online at nationalgeographic.com/books

For librarians and teachers: ngchildrensbooks.org

More for kids from National Geographic: kids.nationalgeographic.com

For information about special discounts for bulk purchases, please contact National Geographic Books Special Sales: ngspecsales@ngs.org

For rights or permissions inquiries, please contact National Geographic Books Subsidiary Rights: ngbookrights@ngs.org

ISBN: 978-1-4263-2199-3
Printed in China

15/RRDS/1